Contents

About the Milky Way Galaxy	**4**
Size	**6**
Shape	**8**
Age	**10**
Stars	**12**
Dust	**14**
Gas	**16**
Planets	**18**
The Central Black Hole	**20**
The Central Bulge	**22**
Clusters	**24**
The Halo	**26**
Our Home Galaxy	**28**
Glossary	30
For More Information	31
Index	32

About the Milky Way Galaxy

Look up on a dark, clear night. See that faint dusting of white stars stretching across the sky? That's the Milky Way galaxy. It's made up of hundreds of billions of stars and clouds of dust and gas. Our Sun is one of those billions of stars. That means Earth and all the other planets of our solar system

On a dark, clear night, the Milky Way is a spectacular sight.

LET'S FIND OUT! SPACE

WHAT IS THE MILKY WAY?

EDWARD WILLETT

Britannica
Educational Publishing
IN ASSOCIATION WITH
ROSEN
EDUCATIONAL SERVICES

Published in 2015 by Britannica Educational Publishing (a trademark of Encyclopædia Britannica, Inc.) in association with The Rosen Publishing Group, Inc.
29 East 21st Street, New York, NY 10010

Distributed exclusively by Rosen Publishing.
To see additional Britannica Educational Publishing titles, go to rosenpublishing.com.

First Edition

Britannica Educational Publishing
J.E. Luebering: Director, Core Reference Group
Mary Rose McCudden: Editor, Britannica Student Encyclopedia

Rosen Publishing
Hope Lourie Killcoyne: Executive Editor
Shalini Saxena: Editor
Nelson Sá: Art Director
Michael Moy: Designer
Cindy Reiman: Photography Manager
Amy Feinberg: Photo Research

Cataloging-in-Publication Data

Willett, Edward, 1959- author.
What is the Milky Way?/Edward Willett. — First edition.
pages cm. — (Let's find out! Space)
Audience: Grades 3-6.
Includes bibliographical references and index.
ISBN 978-1-62275-481-6 (library bound) — ISBN 978-1-62275-483-0 (pbk.) — ISBN 978-1-62275-484-7 (6-pack)
1. Milky Way—Juvenile literature. I. Title.
QB857.7.W55 2015
523.1'13—dc23

2014000810

Manufactured in the United States of America

Photo Credits

Cover, p. 1 (galaxy) Vladimir Arndt/Shutterstock.com; cover, p. 1, interior page borders (sky) nienora/Shutterstock.com; p. 4 Neutronman/iStock/Thinkstock; pp. 5, 9, 12, 17, 26 Encyclopædia Britannica, Inc.; p. 6 Roman Sakhno/iStock/Thinkstock; p. 7 N. Martin & R. Ibata (Strasbourg Observatory, Strasbourg University, CNRS); p. 8 NASA/JPL-Caltech/R. Hurt (SSC); p. 10 Babek Tafreshi/SSPL/Getty Images; p. 11 Courtesy of Palomar Observatory/California Institute of Technology; p. 13 NASA/JPL/California Institute of Technology; p. 14 Courtesy of D. Brownlee, University of Washington; photograph, M. Wheelock; p. 15 NASA, ESA, and Z. Levay (STScI/AURA); p. 16 VLT/ESO; p. 18 NASA/Lunar and Planetary Laboratory; p. 19 NASA/JPL-Caltech/Cornell; p. 20 NASA/CXC/MIT/F.K. Baganoff et al.; p. 21 Walter Jaffe/Leiden Observatory, Holland Ford/JHU/STScI, and NASA; pp. 22, 23 NASA; p. 24 The Hubble Heritage Team (AURA/ STScI/NASA); p. 25 N.A. Sharp–National Optical Astronomy Observatory/Association of Universities for Research in Astronomy/National Science Foundation; p. 27 AURA/STScI/NASA/JPL (NASA photo # STScI-PRC96-10); p. 28 ESO/S. Brunier; p. 29 NASA/NOAA/GSFC/Suomi NPP/VIIRS/Norman Kuring.

Think About It

The Milky Way galaxy is full of dust, as well as stars. With the naked eye, we can see only a few thousand of the galaxy's hundreds of billions of stars. What could be blocking our view?

are also part of the Milky Way.

The galaxy is shaped like a giant pinwheel. We're inside one of the pinwheel's arms. All the stars you see are in our arm or elsewhere in the pinwheel.

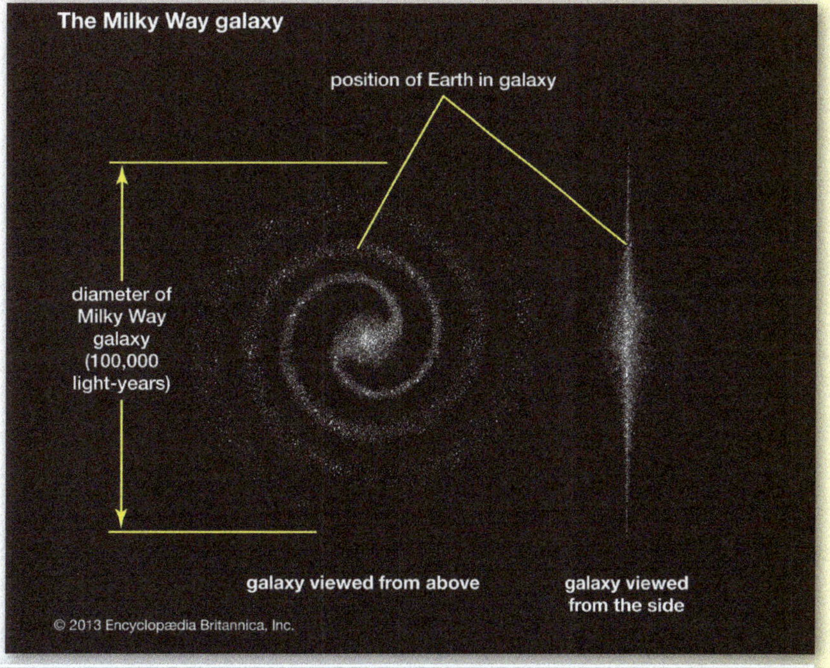

From above, the Milky Way looks like a pinwheel. From the side, it looks like a flat disk with a slightly bulging center.

SIZE

Distances in space are measured in light-years. One light-year is the distance that light travels in a year. The speed of light is about 186,000 miles per second (about 300,000 kilometers per second). That means a light-year is about 5.9 trillion miles, or around 9.5 trillion kilometers.

So how big is the Milky Way galaxy? About 100,000 light-years across. That's 590,000,000,000,000,000 miles!

Our solar system is about 27,000 light-years away from the

Space is so vast that light from the Sun takes more than eight minutes to reach us.

center of the galaxy. The Milky Way is only one of billions of galaxies in the universe. The closest galaxy to the Milky Way is the Canis Major Dwarf Galaxy, discovered in 2003, which our galaxy is tearing apart! It's actually closer to our solar system than the center of our galaxy is.

The Canis Major Dwarf Galaxy is so close to the Milky Way that it is being slowly ripped apart by the Milky Way's gravity.

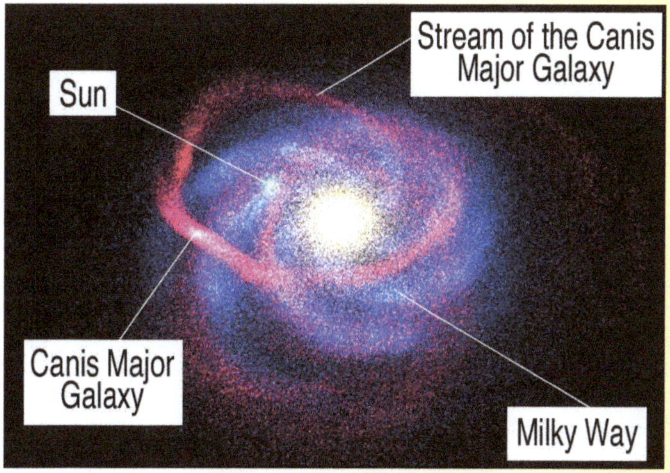

Compare and Contrast

The Canis Major Dwarf Galaxy is about 25,000 light-years from our solar system. Earth is about 27,000 light-years from the center of the Milky Way Galaxy. Is Earth closer to the galactic center of the Milky Way or Canis Major?

Shape

As noted earlier, the Milky Way galaxy is shaped like a pinwheel. We can't see that from Earth. Astronomers have figured out the shape of the galaxy by mapping the movement of stars and hydrogen clouds within the galaxy. The Milky Way has four main spiral arms.

Just as the planets in our solar system revolve around the Sun, everything in the Milky Way rotates around the galaxy's nucleus. It takes about 225 million years for

This artist's rendering shows what the Milky Way galaxy might look like if viewed from above. The arrow marks the location of our Sun.

the Sun to make one complete revolution. This revolving motion is what has given the galaxy its spiral shape.

Galaxies are grouped into three general categories based on their shape: spiral, elliptical, or irregular.

Compare and Contrast

Not all galaxies are spiral like ours. Look at some photographs of galaxies and compare them to the Milky Way. What other shapes do you see?

Age

The oldest stars in the Milky Way are about 13.6 billion years old. This is close to the age of the entire universe, which is estimated at 13.7 billion years.

It's harder to say exactly how old the galaxy is, though, because even after the oldest stars in it were

An amateur astronomer studies the Milky Way galaxy through powerful binoculars.

born, they still had to be drawn together into clusters that in turn joined together to create the Milky Way. As a result, the Milky Way is quite a bit younger than the oldest stars in it. It's estimated that the disk of gas, dust, and stars that surrounds the Milky Way's bar-shaped core region didn't form until about 10 to 12 billion years ago.

Think About It

The Pleiades is a star cluster. These extremely luminous stars formed within the last 100 million years.

The Pleiades is one of the brightest star clusters in the night sky.

STARS

Galaxies are primarily made up of stars. A star is a huge, glowing ball of gas, usually hydrogen. A star is so massive that its enormous gravity changes the hydrogen at the star's core into helium. This process, called fusion, generates an enormous amount of energy that causes the star to shine.

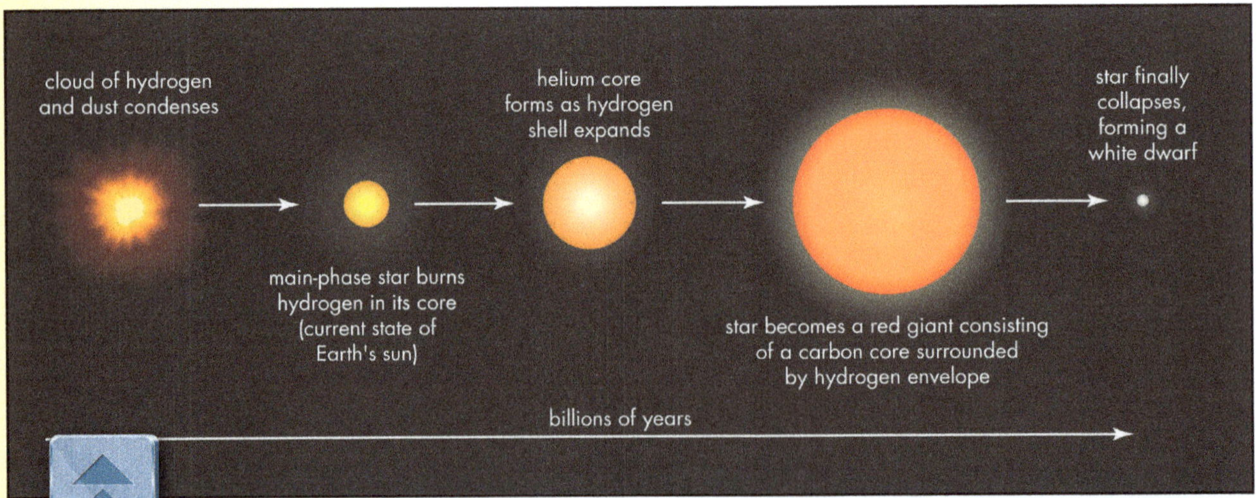

This timeline shows the stages in the life of a medium-sized star.

Compare and Contrast

There are between 200 and 400 billion stars in the Milky Way galaxy. That's a lot, but as galaxies go, it's nothing special. The largest known galaxy, IC 1101, has more than 100 *trillion* stars! How does the Milky Way compare in number of stars to other galaxies?

Stars are being lost to vast explosions called supernovae or collapsing into white dwarfs, but new stars are also being born. The Milky Way grows by about seven stars a year.

This cloud of gas and dust is Cassiopeia A, the remnant of the supernova explosion caused by the collapse of a massive star.

Dust

Another major component of the Milky Way is dust. This dust is so thick between us and the center of the galaxy that we can only see objects up to about 2,000 light-years away. That's only about one-fifteenth of the way to the nucleus.

For the same reason, we can only see the dust clouds closest to us. They can be a million times

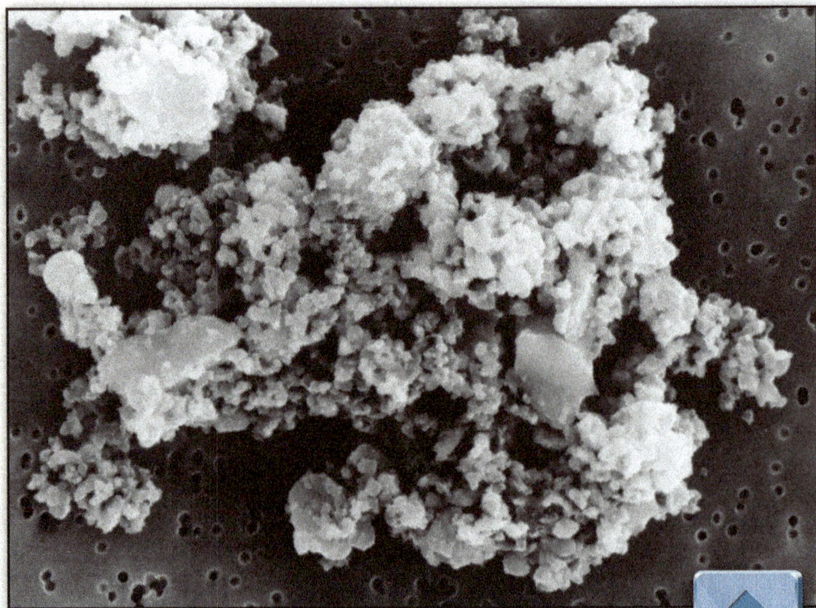

This particle of interplanetary dust was collected in Earth's atmosphere by a NASA high-altitude research aircraft.

THINK ABOUT IT

The Latin name for the Milky Way is *Via Lactea*. That translates as "Road of Milk." Why do you think it's called that?

the mass of the Sun and range in size all the way from just a fraction of a light-year to hundreds of light-years across.

Some of the pale glow that we see when we look at the Milky Way is starlight reflecting off these clouds of dust.

Some of the characteristic yellow-white glow that gives the Milky Way its name is caused by starlight reflecting off clouds of galactic dust.

Gas

In addition to stars and dust, the Milky Way also contains a lot of gas. Gas and dust together are estimated to make up between 10 and 15 percent of the normal matter in the galaxy. The gas is spread very thin among the stars, filling the space between them.

The gas consists mostly of hydrogen. There's a lot of it because the galaxy is so big, but it's very thinly spread. In

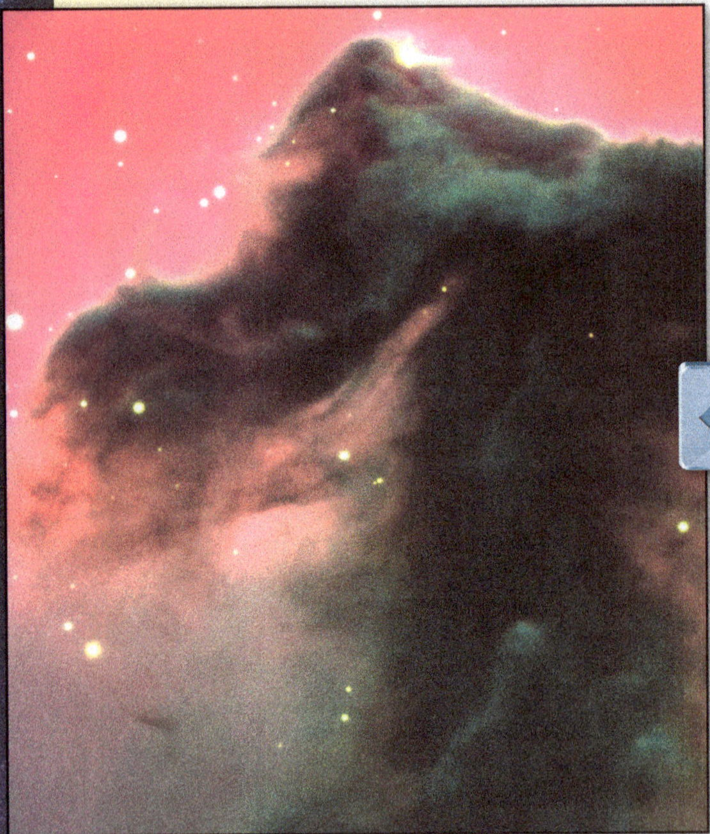

In this photo of the Horsehead Nebula in Orion, which consists of clouds of interstellar dust, the red glowing areas reveal the presence of hydrogen.

fact, near the Sun the average density of interstellar gas is only about one hydrogen atom per cubic centimeter—or about 16 atoms per cubic inch.

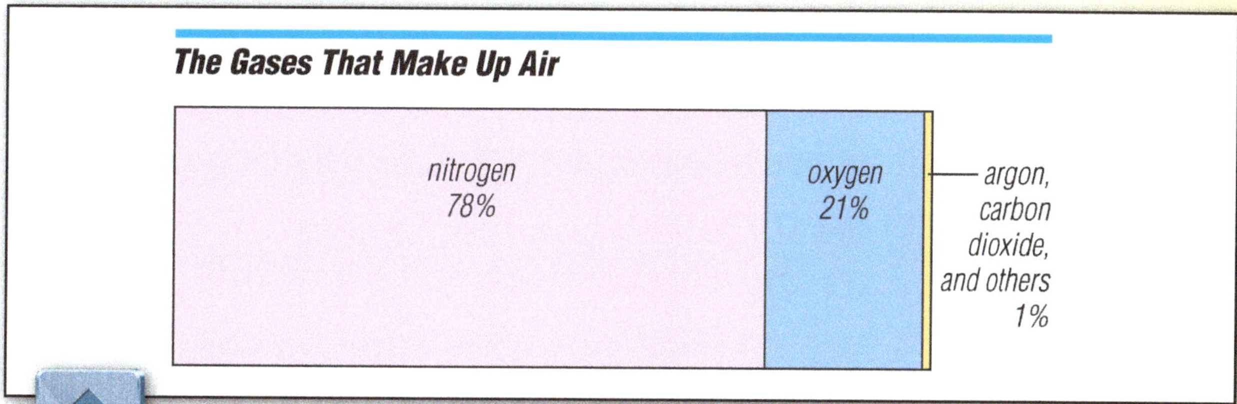

Our atmosphere consists mainly of nitrogen and oxygen, with small amounts of argon and carbon dioxide, and even smaller amounts of hydrogen, neon, krypton, helium, ozone, and xenon.

Compare and Contrast

Just how thin is interstellar hydrogen? Compare it to ordinary air, in which there are 10^{19} air molecules per cubic inch. That's a 1 with 19 zeroes after it!

PLANETS

Our Sun is a star in the Milky Way that is orbited by several planets, including Earth. Many of the other stars in the Milky Way are also orbited by planets. Scientists are not sure how many because they have only been able to detect planets orbiting other stars for about 20 years. However, it appears the number is in the hundreds of billions.

The eight planets of the solar system, scaled to show the approximate sizes of the bodies relative to one another.

Many of those planets are much larger than Earth (like Jupiter) or much colder than Earth (like Mars) or much hotter than Earth (like Venus). But one recent estimate is that there could be as many as 40 billion Earth-sized planets that are about the same temperature as Earth. This means that they could possibly support life!

The surface of Mars, with its cold, thin atmosphere and lack of water, is very different from that of Earth.

Think About It

Earth is the only planet known to have life on it. Do you think it's possible that intelligent life exists on other planets?

The Central Black Hole

At the center of most galaxies there is a massive black hole. The Milky Way is no exception. The black hole at our galaxy's center is named Sagittarius A*. Its mass is about 4.3 million times greater than the Sun's, and it is about 27 million miles (44 million kilometers) across.

This image from the Chandra X-ray Observatory shows the center of the Milky Way galaxy.

We can't see the black hole, but we know it is there. We know it because of rapidly moving gas clouds in the area and because of the infrared radiation being emitted when gas and dust fall into it. As gas nears the black hole, it is squeezed into a rapidly rotating disk. This extends outward somewhere between 5 and 30 light-years from the black hole.

This picture from the Hubble Space Telescope shows a huge ring of gas and dust in another galaxy. Scientists think the ring may surround a black hole.

A **black hole** is a body whose gravity is so strong that nothing can escape it—not even light.

THE CENTRAL BULGE

The main disk of the Milky Way is about 1,000 light-years thick. However, at the center of the galaxy is a peanut-shaped mass of stars that bulges out above and below the disk. Most of the stars in this mass are very old.

An image of the center of the Milky Way galaxy. The yellow and green spots and blobs are giant clouds of interstellar gas and dust.

Although we can't see the center of the galaxy from Earth because of clouds of dust, we can see

Think About It

What would it be like to live on a planet orbiting a star far above or below the disk of the galaxy? What would you see when you looked up at the night sky?

some of the stars in the central bulge because they stick up above and down below the dust.

The space above and below the disk of the galaxy has a thin population of old stars similar to those in the central bulge.

This image shows what the Milky Way galaxy looks like as seen from the side. The central bulge is clearly visible.

CLUSTERS

Although many stars in the Milky Way are either single stars like the Sun or double stars, there are many groups or clusters containing anywhere from tens to thousands of stars.

This is globular cluster M80, which is located 28,000 light-years from Earth and contains hundreds of thousands of stars.

The Milky Way contains more than 150 ball-shaped groups of very old stars called globular clusters. They range from 10 to 300 light-years in diameter.

Open clusters are less tightly organized.

Most are less than 5 light-years in diameter. They are much younger than globular clusters.

Stellar associations are very loose groupings of young stars that all formed at about the same time. They average about 250 light-years in diameter.

This is M7, an open star cluster in the Scorpius constellation.

Double stars are pairs of stars bound to each other by gravity. About half the stars in the Milky Way are double stars.

THE HALO

The Milky Way galaxy contains a lot of matter that we can see, but it contains even more that we can't see.

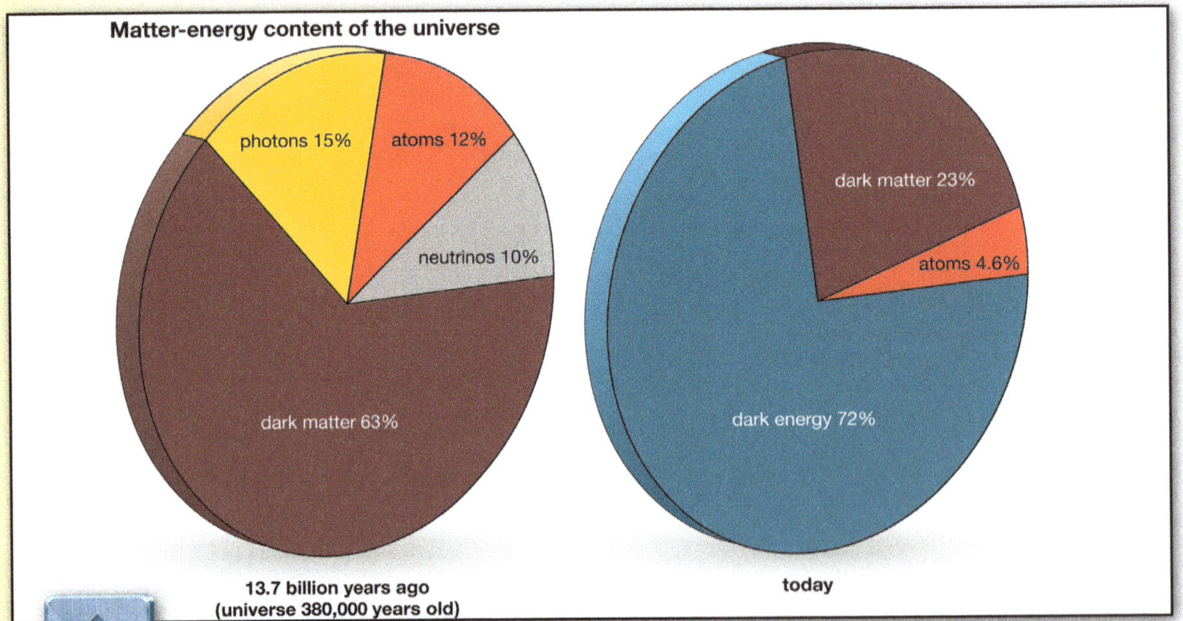

These graphs show how the matter-energy content of the universe has changed over the past 13.7 billion years. The universe is now composed largely of dark energy. This is energy believed to exist throughout space and to be responsible for accelerating the expansion of the universe.

This is called dark matter (because we can't see it), and nobody knows for sure what it is. We only know it exists because of the effect that it has on the galaxy's rotation.

This dark matter forms a massive halo around the galaxy, but we don't know its exact shape or how far it extends. All we know is that it stretches beyond 100,000 light-years from the center, and its mass is several times greater than all the rest of the galaxy!

Although we can't see dark matter, we can detect the effects of its gravity. In this picture, the gravitational field of a galactic cluster about five billion light-years away has bent the light around it.

Think About It

The nature of dark matter is one of the major questions modern astronomers are working to answer. What do you think it might be?

Our Home Galaxy

The next time you look up at that milky glow stretching across the night sky, think about what you're seeing: thousands of stars stretching between you and the center of the Milky Way galaxy, and clouds of dust lit from behind by the billions of stars that you can't see.

It can make you feel very small when you realize that even though the Milky Way galaxy contains hundreds

The Milky Way stretches above the La Silla Observatory, part of the European Southern Observatory in Chile.

of billions of stars and hundreds of billions of planets, it is only one of billions of galaxies in the universe.

But it's the most important galaxy to us because it contains our Sun, our solar system, and our Earth.

For us, the Milky Way is home.

Earth is just a tiny bit of matter in the Milky Way galaxy, which is itself barely a speck in the universe as a whole.

THINK ABOUT IT

Why do you think it's important for us to study the Milky Way and the universe in general?

GLOSSARY

astronomers Scientists who study space.

atom The smallest particle of an element.

galaxy One of the very large groups of stars and other matter that are found throughout the universe.

gravity A force of attraction between particles or bodies that have mass.

helium A colorless gas that is the second most abundant and second lightest element in the universe after hydrogen.

hydrogen A colorless gas that is the most abundant and lightest element in the universe.

infrared radiation A form of electromagnetic radiation that lies just outside the visible spectrum of light at the red end.

light-year The distance that light travels in one year: 5.88 trillion miles (9.46 trillion kilometers).

mass The quantity of matter in an object.

nucleus The central point, group, or mass of something, such as a galaxy.

planets Heavenly bodies other than comets, asteroids, or satellites that travel in orbit around a star.

revolution The time it takes one object to complete an orbit around another object.

solar system The Sun, its eight major planets, the dwarf planets and small bodies, and interplanetary dust and gas under the Sun's gravitational control.

stars Balls of gas of enormous mass that produce their own light.

supernova The explosion of a very large star.

X-ray A very powerful form of electromagnetic radiation that can penetrate or pass through many objects.

For More Information

Books

Farndon, John. *What Do We Know About Stars and Galaxies?* (Freestyle Express: Earth, Space, and Beyond). Houndmills, England: Raintree Publishers, 2011.

Gibbons, Gail. *Galaxies, Galaxies!* New York, NY: Holiday House, 2008.

Kopp, Megan. *Milky Way and Other Galaxies* (Fact Finders: The Solar System and Beyond). North Mankato, MN: Capstone Press, 2011.

Peddicord, Jane Ann. *Night Wonders*. Watertown, MA: Charlesbridge Publishing, 2005.

Vogt, Gregory. *The Milky Way* (Early Bird Astronomy). Minneapolis, MN: Lerner Publishing Group, 2010.

Websites

Because of the changing nature of Internet links, Rosen Publishing has developed an online list of websites related to the subject of this book. This site is updated regularly. Please use this link to access the list:

http://www.rosenlinks.com/lfo/milky

Index

astronomers, 8, 10, 27
atoms, 17

black holes, 20–21

Canis Major, 7

dark matter, 26–27
double stars, 24, 25
dust, 4, 5, 11, 13–15, 16, 21-23, 28

Earth, 4, 7, 8, 14, 18, 19, 22, 24, 29

fusion, 12

galaxies, categories of, 9
gases, 4, 11, 12, 13, 16–17, 21, 22
gravity, 7, 12, 21, 25, 27

helium, 12, 17
hydrogen, 8, 12, 16, 17
IC 1101, 13

infrared radiation, 21

Jupiter, 19

Mars, 19
Milky Way
- age, 10–11
- central bulge, 22–23
- clusters, 11, 24–25, 27
- our home galaxy, 28–29
- overview, 4–5
- shape, 8–9
- size, 6–7

nebula, 16

observatories, 20, 28

planets, 4, 8, 14, 18–19, 23, 29

revolutions, 9
Sagittarius A*, 20

solar systems, 4, 7, 8, 18, 29
stellar associations, 25
supernovae, 13

universes, 7, 10, 26, 29

Venus, 19
Via Lactea, 15